M000079085

A BORN LEADER

A BORN LEADER

(I Always Knew I was Born to Lead)

CYNTHIA SKIEF

A BORN LEADER

Copyright © 2019 by Cynthia Skief. All rights reserved.

Scripture quotations noted KJV are from the King James Version of the Holy Bible.

No part of this publication may be reproduced, stored in a retrieval system or transmitted in any way by any means, electronic, mechanical, photocopy, recording or otherwise without the prior permission of the author except as provided by USA copyright law.

CONTENTS

INTRODUCTION

I began writing these words about my journey as a leader during the time when members of my congregation, New Life Worship Center in Tyler Texas, were embarking upon a 21-day fast. Fasting together was one of our church's annual activities, and I always looked forward to them. Personally, it allows for me to gain deeper spiritual insight and to simply rededicate myself to carrying on the work of Christ. I not only abstain from some of my favorite foods, sweets, breads, and pasta but restrict my interactions with so many of life's unnecessary distractions. I simply focus on myself and family and take part in deeper and more personal conversations with God. By asking God to more clearly reveal my life's purpose, I'm able to draw up a roadmap for the entire year ahead.

Often times, I will spend time on the sofa with my bible and a note pad, reading and writing what I sense the Holy Spirit is saying to me at the moment. I journal each day, and there will be scriptures I'll recite to remind me of the awesome presence of God in my life. Once I've completed a fast, I am empowered with a renewed spirit and mind to continue my life's journey into the new year.

This particular fast was unique, however. While reading Jentezen Franklin's book, *Fasting: Opening the Door to a Deeper, More Intimate, More Powerful Relationship With God*, I grabbed a notebook and began writing about an aspect of my life that I hadn't previously contemplated at any measurable depth. For three days and four nights, I reflected on my journey as a leader, which began during the early childhood of my humble beginnings in Winona Texas. After three days of writing, the draft was finished, and I sat down at my computer, typed it, and saved as "Born-Leader".

Over the years, I've occasionally considered sharing it with others, but each time decided not to. However, in September of 2002, I was attending a Bible study held by Barbara Sandiford. After praying for me, she opened the Bible and read, "Lord gave the word: great was the company of those that published it." (Psalm 68:11) She then handed me a copy of John Maxwell's book *17 Disputable Laws of Teamwork* and wrote the following inside the book's jacket:

My dear friend, Cynthia, I love your vision, your passion, your strategy. May the Holy Spirit energize each of your leaders to run with the vision. I pray for you and bless you, [a] woman of God called for such a time as this. [We are] Co-Laborers together in Christ.

–Love from Barbara Sandiford

I thanked her and began to walk away with a renewed spirit. "Cynthia," she firmly declared, waiting until we were again facing each other, "*You* are going to be a great leader and will be a writer who publishes books." Barbara and her husband, Roy, are still active leaders with the Youth with a Mission (YWAM) in Tyler. I'm not sure whether she knew entirely, but her words touched my heart in a profound way, and I believe that was the moment this book was conceptualized.

Still, perhaps it wasn't the right time, but I knew then that I was a born leader; leading is what I've done for most of my life. It would be another 2 decades, again, while fasting, that I made a decision to publish this book.

ACKNOWLEDGEMENT

"Honour thy father and thy mother: that thy days may be long upon the land which the Lord thy God giveth thee." (Exodus 20:12)

I want to thank my family for all the important life lessons I've learned along the way. There have been many hard times, too many to recount, but, "The righteous cry, and the Lord heareth, and delivereth them out of all their troubles." (Psalm 34:17) There were many days I cried, but when I called on him, he answered me and delivered me out of all my troubles. I honor my mother, Patricia Gladys Price Cooper, and my father, the late Phillip Cooper, Jr., for the extraordinary leadership qualities they invested in me as a child. Early on, they empowered and propelled me toward my destiny to become the leader that I am today. They were not aware of the assignment given to them as parents, yet their obedience to God, the sacrifices they made, the manner in which they trained me, and their unconditional love were all the necessary ingredients God ordained. I am forever grateful. I wasn't easy raising but thank you for your patience and endurance. You molded me into a great leader for the world today. Thank you for being my parents.

I want to thank my husband, Archie, and our two lovely children, Shayla and Cameron, who have been on the sidelines watching and wondering at times how problem after problem would eventually work out for our good. My family has seen the good, bad, and ugly of my character, yet we have grown and developed as leaders together. They have not only learned from me, they have encouraged, inspired, and motivated me to hang in there as a leader. They have encouraged me to put those shoulders back, and to keep on walking with the knowledge that they have my back.

I want to thank my siblings, Karen, Anthony, and Robbie, for allowing me to lead them, for it was my first time, and they made it easy. It's not often people are blessed with siblings who simply know how to follow, respect, and love the leader so unconditionally. I was blessed to start with an easy team. To God be the glory for all the things He has done and is getting ready to do in my life.

CHAPTER ONE

· · · · · · ● ● ● ● ● ⬤ ● ● ● ● ● · · ·

The Leader Inside

"O God, thou hast taught me from my youth: and hitherto have I declared thy wondrous works."
(Psalm 71:17)

"Why don't you get somewhere and 'sat' down?"

"You talk too much!"

"Stop talking so much!"

"Get somewhere and 'sat' down!"

As a child growing up in Winona Texas, these words rang loudly and became a daily song for me. It's funny, though, because no matter how hard you try, you can never shut a born leader up or down. Leaders don't wait for a conversation from people; leaders generate the conversation. I would get somewhere and "sat" down for a little while but kept on running my mouth even when I was sitting down. It would take many years, once I had matured spiritually, for me to realize the enemy was trying to hide the gift God had given me.

Although I was born to lead, I didn't know for sure until I was around five years old. It was a hot summer day in 1964, and there I was, a small child, weighing only about 60 pounds, standing on a wash tub staring down at the dishes in a large pan for the very first time. There were two tubs; one was used for washing the dishes while the other was for rinsing the dishes. I had been asking my mother for months to help with the chores and was also eager to sweep the floors and dust the furniture. Mama taught me these chores at a very early age and made me feel special, but what I didn't know was that once learned, my responsibilities would continue to increase each year of my life.

With all that was going on in the world in December of 1964, my only dream was to own a doll that walked and talked like a real person. My sister Karen and I imagined owning dolls with soft skin for us to hold and authentic hair for us to comb. Our fantasies had no boundaries. Christmas was approaching, and I envisioned Santa delivering our dolls sometime between midnight and the break of dawn. We already had enough of those fake dolls that never did anything but stare at you without blinking. We figured it was time for the real McCoy's. So, on Christmas Eve, Karen and I turned in early so we could rise early and open our gifts—we might even catch a glimpse of Santa making the delivery.

We didn't spot Santa, but we received lots of presents, including large dolls that were just about as tall as us. The only problem was that they were harder than metal, and their eyes and mouths didn't move. When you think of it, even their hair didn't seem all that real. It only took a split second for me to think, *these are not exactly what I had in mind, but maybe it's a joke.* My mind was fixed on something real, something that could talk, walk, and act like a real person. Although disappointed, I was grateful and played with the dolls for a little while.

Shortly after opening up our gifts, Karen and I were told by Dad to come into the bedroom because he wanted to show us something. I supposed, *Hmmm, maybe Santa had placed the dolls in their room by mistake.* But to our everlasting surprise, we were introduced to our new baby brother! Anthony Quinn Cooper was born on December 25, 1964, precisely around the time I envisioned Santa delivering our presents. It would be the first of many of my dreams to come true. Anthony was our Christmas baby! I had inherited a real live, soft and cuddly baby brother with eyes that moved and a mouth that made noises. Even Anthony's pale skin color was very similar to those dolls we received for Christmas. At first, I thought my mother must have received the wrong baby because he looked nothing like us! He had pale, reddish skin and piercing green eyes. He was a funny looking baby boy, but we embraced him with love, and that Christmas turned out to be the best ever, particularly for Karen, who ended up with two dolls that year.

I immediately began helping Mama take care of Anthony but got off to a rocky start. I would follow her example of how to hold him. She would lay him across her lap, and I would try emulating her, yet time after time, I would drop him, and he would hit the floor, crying every time. That didn't stop me from wanting to continue helping her take care of him, it just meant having to be reminded over and over again, "You're the big sister, and it's time for you to start acting like one." There were many days I didn't want to hear that. After all, I was still a child, and I wanted to be patted and babied from time to time, myself. It didn't take long for me to realize that Karen and Anthony were getting all the attention.

Every night, my mama would sit at the end of our bed and recite the Lord's prayer. I learned to recite the prayer at the age of five and taught it to my sister soon after. And when Anthony started to talk, Karen and I began teaching it to him so he could pray with us. After we all learned the Lord's prayer, my mama taught us Psalm 23 (If you have small children, teach them how to recite both the Lord's Prayer and Psalm 23 because they teach us how to pray and maintain faith).

Every night we would recite our prayers and scripture, and afterwards Karen and I would have fun laughing in bed. I would make Karen laugh, yet she knew how to chuckle without our parents hearing her. This wasn't the case with me, as I was always getting us into trouble by laughing too loudly. Mama and Daddy would repeat many times throughout the night, "Girls, stop that laughing and go to sleep!" Looking back, it's a wonder my parents ever got any sleep at night.

My mother would call both Karen and I Baby, and it would be confusing at times. Sometimes, when I was helping with the chores, I would ask, "If I'm your baby, why am I doing the chores?" Again, she would remind me that I was the big sister and it was time for me to act like one. In hindsight, I now realize my Mama was kicking me out of the comfort nest because it was my time to fly.

Karen was two years younger than me, and like Anthony, she was a December baby, born on the 13th. She and I were very close to each other and did everything together. We played together, read together, and even held hands wherever we went. I even taught Karen how to ride a bicycle, and whatever my Mama taught me to do, she would always encourage me to teach Karen. We enjoyed spending so much time together, and growing up, we were inseparable.

Our parents didn't allow us to fight with each another. In fact, Karen and I only fought one time, and I still have proof. During our fight, she dug her long finger nails so deeply into my skin that I still have the scar. So, yes, I would like to think my parents played a part in keeping us from fighting, but there were more practical reasons to not fight my sister. Being a habitual nail-biter, I didn't have nails. Karen was very shy and quiet, so people thought she was timid and couldn't fight, but there was a tiger inside of her. On the other hand, I was the big talker, and that hasn't changed.

Since I was the oldest, babysitting invariably fell upon my shoulders. I would have to entertain all the children that came to visit our home while Karen would only have to sit beside me laughing at everything I said. I was quite the entertainer, though, and this sometimes landed me into big trouble. My mama always took us to church, and when I misbehaved, she would give me the glare, which in hindsight actually saved me from many whippings. Although I was quite a jokester, I always knew to immediately straighten up and stop playing around.

I started leading around the home at age five, and it was also when I told my mama that Karen and I wanted to be baptized. Mama agreed, and on a bitter and cold Sunday night at Mt. Olive Missionary Baptist Church in Winona, Texas, we were finally immersed into the frigid water. In fact, it was so cold, I was scared to death of freezing. I remember the pastor saying, "I baptize you in the name of the Father, the Son, and the Holy Spirit," as my little shivering body clung to him tightly. I tried, with all the strength I could muster, to climb out of the water, but the pastor literally snatched me from the wall back into that cold water. Once baptized, I was even more terrified. I wanted to run and tell everybody that they really didn't want to get baptized. It's fair to say that my first baptism was not a pleasant experience. Fortunately, I was baptized again in October 2003, and glory to God, joy filled my soul the second time around.

My dad taught me how to drive his old 1957 stick shift Chevrolet truck when I was seven years old. While other kids in my community were playing with toy trucks and animals, I was driving my dad's truck and riding horses. As I got older, my cousin would brag about me to the kids at school, and my dad, also very proud, would invite his riding buddies over on the weekends where he, too, would brag about my skills. He'd often tell me to get the horse out of the pasture, saddle up, and ride down the street so his buddies could see how smart and gifted I was. That was not fun for me; it was work!

But I soon learned to love driving and riding my favorite horse, King. He was a spoiled horse who always knew when I was about to feed, bathe, or get him out of the pasture. When we would head towards the pasture, he would acknowledge our presence by nodding his head and kicking his hooves into the sand. He was part of the family, but after my dad passed away in 1980, it became difficult to take care of him. For a while, my grandfather, Papa Dee, would help us feed the horses every day, but I'll never forget the day we finally had to sell them and the cows. That had to be one of the saddest days of my life.

On the weekends, my dad would teach me how to drive. Interstate 20, the stretch of highway between Dallas and Louisiana, was our testing ground. He would tell me to watch out for other drivers, especially the big trucks. He taught me very well because, to this very day, my family and friends tell me all the time how great a driver I am. There have been many days I have had to help people parallel park or back their vehicles into a tight spot because they did not know how to do it. More importantly, he taught me how to read road maps and not to depend on others for directions. "You could end up in Callow Mezzo," he'd would often say, as if there really was such a place.

Because my dad taught me how to drive and fix automobiles, I've driven around the United States without fear of huge trucks, engine problems, and dangerous highways. Today, road trips are a family passion, and I'm the family's designated driver and self-appointed navigator. I know that my husband, Archie, has always trusted my driving abilities and skills at navigation because he's always nodded off as soon as he's settled in the vehicle. Since I did not have the patience to teach Shayla or Cameron how to drive, that task fell on him. Yet, he's wide awake when either of the two are driving. After a long day on the road, I often think my dad is probably with the heavenly host smiling down on me and saying, "That's my girl, that's the way I taught you."

One experience I'll never forget was a trip to Richmond Virginia I took with my church. We traveled there on a bus to attend the National Baptist Convention. My father had recently taught me to read maps, and I knew this trip afforded me the opportunity to apply my knowledge. So, when we stopped at a rest area, I made my way to the bus driver to ask what route he was taking. "I brought my map along and wanted to follow," I told him. He looked quite amazed. It was late at night, and everyone on the bus was getting tired, dozing off one by one, until all you could hear was one or two people snoring. But little Cynthia was wide awake, neither tired nor sleepy. I retrieved my flashlight, pointed it toward the map, and began following the bus route to Virginia.

As I compared the road signs with my map and took in the scenery, I began to wonder whether I was really awake or simply dreaming. Signs that didn't align with the map, and locations on the map that didn't seem to connect with our locality, began appearing at random. *Maybe I missed something Dad taught me,* I wondered. But I assumed the bus driver knew where he was taking us. I figured I must have nodded off and decided to go to sleep like everyone else and catch up with the navigation the following morning.

We stopped for breakfast early in the morning, but I managed to find the bus driver to ask him where we were headed so I could get back on track. "I got off a little bit, but I think we are going to make up the time in about an hour," he said somewhat dismissively. I pulled out my map and asked him to show me exactly where were on *my* map. After he pointed to where we were located, I explained to him that we would not make up time in an hour—we were approximately 3 hours off the route. I notified the trip's coordinator, who after having a few words with the bus driver, asked, "Young lady, do you know how to get us back on track?"

"Sure do," I responded confidently. With that, the trip's coordinator notified the bus driver he would be taking directions from me and informed the congregation that we would be arriving at our destination in three hours. Sure enough, three hours later, we arrived in Richmond Virginia. Upon arrival, the relieved coordinator asked, "Young lady, who taught you how to read maps?"

"My daddy!" I proudly responded.

I began working at a very early age, but I was about 9 years old when I realized I was no longer simply doing chores. I was feeding the dogs, cows, horses, and the hogs. I began to complain to my grandfather, Papa Dee, that my dad was working me far too hard as a child, so he'd defend me from time to time, but that did not help. By the time I became a teenager, I was hauling hay, raking the yard, washing cars, busting fire wood, and loading and unloading pulp wood right alongside my dad. I even drove the loaded pulp wood truck with timber and our big John Deer tractor. But none of this killed me because I was a tomboy in every sense of the word.

In fact, working with my dad caused me to spend lots of time having conversations with God. He would sometimes ask, "Cynthia, who are you talking to?" I would never answer him, but I think he eventually figured it out because afterwards I would sometimes talk to him about God. I remember many days crying out to God to deliver me from those woods. I made many promises to God, one of which was if he would deliver me, I'd work for him all the days of my anointed life.

Whether it was hot, rainy, cold, freezing, storming, or windy, we worked tirelessly in those woods. Although I learned to work hard and developed a great work ethic, it was in those woods that I learned to pray. God was preparing me for my destiny. I didn't realize it at the time, but I do now, that if we can go through the physical seasons, God will help us through our spiritual seasons in life.

On numerous occasions, Dad and I would load two trucks with timber, and I would have to drive the loaded one. He would always ask, "You got this?" I could tell that even though he had confidence in me, he was still cautious. "Cynthia, I need for you to focus," he'd always tell me. My dad would take the lead, and I would trail him in the stick shift loaded with timber. When we would enter a hill, he would signal to me when to shift gears by holding his hand out the window; that's how I knew to shift gears. Every time we would arrive at the wood yard, he would walk to my truck and say, "Cynt, you did well!"

He would go into the wood yard office to get someone to come measure our trucks, but the men never realized I was a girl because my hair was hidden under a cap, and I wore work boots. I must have looked like a boy because I could hear the men asking my dad, "What's your son's name?" They'd tell him, "Phillip your son sure does know how to drive that loaded truck. You've got yourself a good worker. Your boy looks like you, Phillip."

My dad always found humor in these comments, but I didn't. So, one day, I decided that as soon as my dad entered the wood yard office, I would take my cap off and just let my hair hang down (I had very long ponytails tucked under that cap). With my hair on full display, I stepped out of the truck so that everyone could see that I was, in actuality, a girl. At first, this created quite a scene, and my dad was not at all happy about it. But I did it every time the opportunity presented itself. After a couple times, I caught the attention of a young man who would come over and talk with me. Although I thought it was funny, my father didn't. As far as my father was concerned, I may have worked like a boy, but at the end of the day I was a hard-working girl.

When Archie and I moved to Houston in February of 2013, I drove a huge Penske truck loaded with all of our furniture and belongings, as well as our car attached to the rear. I was not afraid, and when we stopped to gas up along the way, I received jaw dropping looks from everyone because Archie was just sitting in the truck looking very comfortable. My dad empowered me to be a fearless traveler, and I am forever grateful to him for that. He also taught me an important leadership skill that I have continued to develop: It takes a visionary to effectively plan from A to Z. I love my dad for that.

My dad taught me how to change the engine oil for our cars and trucks, as well as change flat tires. I've changed a few strangers' tires in my life time, and, yes, that includes the tires of a few men, too! He was a Mechanic, and I would assist him by handing him the correct tools. To effectively do this job, I had to learn all the tools and engine parts. If I would hand him the wrong tool, I'd have to listen to him say, "Cynt, focus!"

Once, after my dad had passed away, my engine ran hot, and the vehicle stopped on me. By then, I was accustomed to solving car problems on my own. So, there I stood, removing that hot cap off the radiator. At some point, a gentleman pulled up next to my vehicle to offer assistance.

"Can I help?" the guy politely asked.

"I got it."

As I flipped the trunk open to get a towel, I explained to him that my engine had run hot. Without missing a beat, I took the water jug from my trunk and talked to him while waiting for the engine to cool down. He stood there the entire time observing and learning. He was good company, but more importantly, I was able to teach him how to handle the situation. "Always be prepared," I told him, pointing out the need to have your vehicle stocked with the proper tools, such as gas jugs filled with gas, lug and jack, and a water jug, just in case. Today, most people take roadside assistance for granted and never even consider having the proper tools inside their vehicles. They simply call AAA, assuming they'll always be there for them in case of emergencies. I am not bragging on myself; I am bragging on how my dad was obedient to God by instilling these significant leadership skills into my life.

Not long after Archie and I started dating, he visited my house. I was changing my engine oil, and he asked if he could help. I gave him the wrench to take the oil cap off so he could release the old oil from the engine and went inside to get us some Kool-aide (Archie loved red Kool-aide). But when I returned, I noticed a different type of red liquid emerging from beneath my vehicle. Although I knew the answer, I immediately asked, "What cap did you take off from under my car?" He looked puzzled. That was the last time I allowed him to perform any mechanical work on a vehicle of ours. I gave him the Kool-aide to drink while I retrieved extra cans of transmission fluid to put back in my vehicle and changed the oil.

One of my favorite songs as a child was *Yes, Jesus Loves Me*. Hot or cold, rain or snow, I would sing this song at the top of my lungs. "Yes, Jesus loves me, yes Jesus loves me!" I'd scream. Dad would yell, "Girl, it's time to take a break for lunch!" One day, as I retrieved my lunch from the truck, Dad asked me what I was singing about. I replied, "Yes, Jesus loves me, and he loves you, too!" He asked me to sing it for him, so I grabbed a stick to represent a microphone. Dad laughed and asked, "What's the stick for? I told him it was my microphone, and from then on, when I sang for him, I would use a stick to represent a microphone.

My dad told me so many things that didn't make sense when I was a child, and sometimes he'd say things that I would despise, such as, "Just do what I say, and don't ask why!" However, today, I now realize that many of the things he said to me were "wisdom nuggets." One of my favorites was, "People will only like you as long as they can control you." My dad is my hero. He never attended church with us, and, as a child, I was often conflicted about his choice not to, but as I matured spiritually, I realized that God was using me to minister to him.

I have learned that leading is not controlling another person. When leaders are controlling, they are trying to lead through intimidation. If employees are being led through intimidation, you don't have to worry about them ever asking questions. For sure, I might not have always asked my dad questions, but he was just that, "My daddy." I don't think children are showing up for work searching for their daddies. No one is attending church in search of their daddy, are they? I believe that if you love people like they are your children, they will follow you everywhere you lead. But never ever treat people like they are your children. What you give out is what you will receive in return. If you sow love, you will reap love. If you sow disrespect, well, don't expect love. I have had people say to me, "I thought you were a Christian" simply because I didn't show them love after they disrespected me. I have heard it being said over and over again "Don't dish it out if you can't take it! Nobody ever deserves to be stepped on and then respond in love. A leader sets the standard, establishes boundaries, communicates what they expect, and then they lead by example.

CHAPTER TWO

A Leader in Transition

"And thou shalt teach them diligently unto thy children, and shalt talk of them when thou sittest in thine house, and when thou walkest by the way, and when thou liest down, and when thou risest up." (Deuteronomy 6:7)

The summer of 1971 was one of the hottest. What I remember most, however, was my mama's belly getting so big. She told me I was going to have another sister or brother to take care of. My heart swelled with joy and excitement, and I began to pray that our new baby would be born on my birthday, August 16th. However, Robbie Lanell Cooper decided to have her own birthday and was born on August 21, 1971.

I was full of excitement on the way to the hospital with my dad to the hospital to see my new baby sister. But I will never forget the feeling I had seeing that baby in the hospital. Everyone was saying how beautiful my little baby sister was, but I simply couldn't find anything redeeming. I was not happy, and even remember asking my cousins, "Do you think she is cute?" They all agreed that my baby sister was beautiful.

I braced myself for the moment my parents would bring her home. *There's no way I'm going to be able to love this not-so-cute baby sister the way I know she's supposed to be loved,* I thought. When my parents arrived, I gathered the nerves to take a peek inside the blanket she was wrapped in and screamed, "That's not the baby I saw in the hospital!" I was overcome with joy, as I must have been focusing on a different baby at the hospital. Indeed, she was just like everyone else described her—beautiful! I'd ended up helping Mom to take care of her, too. Naturally, my mama reminded me how to feed her, burp her, change her diapers, comb her hair, dress her, and of course to behave like a big sister.

I spent many days taking care of my siblings but didn't consider babysitting a chore. I found great joy in spoiling and taking care of them, and in truth, I sometimes felt like their mother. Sure, there were times I felt like my childhood was passing me by, that my time was being consumed by too many chores that adults were supposed to do. But, I truly loved children and especially my brother and sisters.

I loved the responsibility of nurturing and taking care of those babies. I could teach potty-training within one week, and this included them knowing the process of how to go to the bathroom and wash their hands. However, once they reached the toddler stage, they were on their own. I would be done with them and grab the next new baby to come along.

As a teenager, I was always looking for a family member's baby to hold, and often asked to take them home with me after church. I loved babies! I thought I was a little mama at the church and would act like those women at church who had babies. Babies I took care of hardly ever cried while they were with me because I knew how to take care of them. It got to the point where people brought crying babies to me to take care of, knowing they knew I could be counted on to keep their children if they had something to do immediately after church, or just needed a break. Most teens these days would not view taking care of babies as fun, but I did, and it even made attending church fun.

Before I married Archie, I asked him whether he loved children because I knew if he didn't, there was going to be a problem. When we got married, there would be children at our place every weekend. On one Easter weekend, I kept five girls. We shopped, made Easter baskets, prepared meals (McDonald's was their favorite place), prepared clothes for church, combed hair—and this was my newborn's first Easter Sunday. Yes, even with my newborn, Shayla, I still enjoyed keeping children.

I never had to spank any of the children because I spoiled them. They understood that if they misbehaved, I had a harsher punishment for them. I would simply take them to their real home. My baby sister Robbie and I laugh about this now. She often says, "Sis, it was that look and the tone of your voice."

Every year, the youth leaders of the church would assign us speeches to recite for Easter and Christmas. My mama would teach us our speeches every year. She was a great reader and taught us to read and spell at an early age. We did not struggle with literacy because my mother exhibited a lot of patience with us in this regard. So, we would quickly learn our speeches and recite them to our parents every day until we had mastered them. She taught us how to enunciate our words correctly and to recite our speeches with action. Yet, no matter how many times we recited our speeches at home, I could never recite my speech without crying in front of the congregation. All I could see were unfriendly faces staring down at me.

People would encourage me by saying, "Cynthia, you did a good job. You just got nervous." But I often felt like Moses when he said, "O my Lord, I am not eloquent, neither heretofore, nor since thou hast spoken unto thy servant: but I am slow of speech, and of a slow tongue." (Exodus 4:10) I always had something to say except when delivering Easter and Christmas speeches. I was great at interpersonal conversations but speaking in front of the entire church congregation was for anyone else but myself. I was once again being pushed out of the comfortable nest.

I would always have to tell my dad about the Easter and Christmas programs at church, and it was always the same story: I cried before reciting my speech. One year, he asked me, "What are you crying about?" "The faces staring at me," I replied. He then told me to stop thinking of them as unfriendly faces but to imagine them smiling at you. "You'll be able to complete your speech if you do this," he said. I thought to myself, *Dad, if you would just attend church with your family!*

Like Moses, I was very young when I began to plead with God to spare me of my purpose in life. I was not a good speaker and was frightened to death of standing in front of people. My knees would shake, and my heart would beat so hard I could hear it myself. I often wondered whether other people could also hear my heart beating so fast and loud. Nevertheless, when God calls you, he will provide. Even today, I sometimes get nervous speaking before a crowd, but I now tell myself, "I can do all things through Christ which strengtheneth me." (Philippians 4:13) Doing so always works for me.

Although my dad never attended church, he conveyed a great deal of wisdom to me, and he led by example. He was the head of our home, and my mama was the nurturer. They were both hard workers and provided for our family, but I had to have tough skin because they were very firm and strict. The tone of their voices and that glare in their eyes spoke volumes and would make you feel like you had just suffered through a whipping without them lifting a finger. My dad would often use the phrase, "Say what you mean and mean what you say." And you better believe that both my parents were never confused about what they said to us. They didn't hold back on how they felt about anything.

Of course, on the flip side, we couldn't express how we felt about anything. It was hard, but on several occasions, I had to hold my peace. As a teen, I would have never told anyone what I've written in this book. I may have thought I knew everything but kept my ideas to myself around them.

Do you know any teenagers who think they know everything? They're probably leaders on the horizon. They just need to be heard.

Although they were fiercely strict, my mama and dad were my best friends growing up. Still, I was very careful what I told them about my experiences at school. For example, I couldn't tell my dad about how the girls at school hated me and how they would bully me because he'd say to me, "If you let them beat you up, you will get another beating when you get home." My mama, the gentler one, would just say, "Stop worrying about what those girls are saying." So, I learned to pick and choose what experiences I shared with them because I didn't want to upset either one. This balancing act was easier said than done, but I survived!

My dad would often say "You probably don't appreciate us now, but one day you will." I didn't fully appreciate my parents then, but I do appreciate every ounce of discipline and love I received from them. At the time, I never agreed with all of those whippings and stupid rules, but they didn't kill me. My parents actively used the scripture, "He that spareth his rod hateth his son; But he that loveth him chasteneth him betimes." (Proverbs 13:24) In other words, "If you refuse to discipline your children, it proves you don't love them;

if you love your children, you will be prompt to discipline them." My parents must have really loved me because they were great disciplinarians, and they knew all the scriptures to support every whipping. Everyone has a choice as to how they raise their children, but I know as a parent, discipline is a guide for development.

The 1978-1977 school year should have been an awesome ending! It was my senior year, and I made the varsity cheerleading team, was voted Most School Spirit by my peers, and my drama teacher selected me to direct the school's drama production. If I could only say one thing about my teachers, it would be that they believed in me, and I would have to add that they spoke life into their students. Even though I had previously hated science and dreaded the moment I would have to dissect a frog, my science teacher knew how to make me love attending his class. Admittedly, though, I survived dissecting the frog by simply delegating that task to my lab partners. I even had a great basketball Coach who was an awesome encourager. It was the love those teachers gave to us in that small, east Texas town of Winona that inspired me to be all that I could as a student. However, I believe it all began at home. Yes, I have shared with you all the chores I had to do, but did I mention I held a full-time job at age 12. My parents had taught me how to multi-task, work under pressure, not stress, prioritize my workload, delegate, focus, communicate and how to meet deadlines. When I graduated from high school, I was ready for college.

CHAPTER THREE

Skill Set in Process

"Train up a child in the way he should go: and when he is old, he will not depart from it." (Proverbs 22:6)

I t was the best of times; it was the worst of times. I had just completed my sophomore year at Jarvis Christian College in Hawkins Texas and was looking forward to the summer. But my family and I were attending a regular Sunday morning church service at Mt. Olive when about an hour into worship, I heard someone pounding on the backdoor, which was located immediately behind the choir stand. Our choir was singing loudly, but somehow, I heard the noise and answered the door. And there stood a Winona constable, looking very serious, as if he was about to deliver some bad news.

"Can I help you?" I asked, realizing something must be wrong for a white man to be standing at the back of our church at 11 o'clock on a Sunday morning.

"I am looking for Phillip Cooper Jr's family," he said, still looking serious.

"I'm his daughter; can I help you?"

He asked if my mother was available so that he could speak with our family. I went to get my mother and my siblings. He told us that my dad had been in an accident. What I thought was fatal was a miracle because my dad actually survived the accident. He had a tumor on his brain, which caused him to have a seizure and lose control of his truck. He lived another nine months and passed away on April 18, 1980.

Our family was devastated, and there was a major shift of leadership in our home. My mama took that role, and with God's grace, we never missed a beat. As the oldest child, a lot of responsibility for raising my siblings fell upon my shoulders. My Mama was working the nightshift at the University of Texas Health Center, so I was in charge of making sure my siblings ate supper, performed chores, and completed their homework. I never disciplined them. Instead, every chance I got, I spoiled them. And, if this was going to continue, I needed to get a job. My mama never asked me to get one, but I was already accustomed to working early hours and late nights with my dad. Again, how else was I going to do what I loved most, spoiling my siblings?

It was raining cats and dogs on the day I went job hunting, but I didn't allow the weather to deter me. After all, I had toughed out worst storms in my life. As I entered the city of Tyler, I noticed a large building with a huge sign that read, Delta Drilling. I had no idea what type of company it was but parked my car, and despite the rain, exited the car and entered the building soaking wet.

"Did you notice it was storming and raining outside?" asked the receptionist, making no effort to conceal her laughter.

"I want to apply for a job," I answered, pretending not to notice her sarcasm. "I did notice, ma'am, thank you."

She telephoned the HR Manager and told him a young lady downstairs wanted to fill out an application for employment. The HR Manager hurried down the elevator to greet me, then escorted me to the Human Resources Department. There he handed me an application to fill out, and after a few seconds of skimming through my resume looked up and asked, "Cynthia, what type of work are you looking for? You have *so* little skills and just a student work study and 2 years of education?"

"I want the type of job with my so-little-skills and qualifications," I answered, thinking to myself, *Cynthia, why?* To my surprise, he laughed.

"Young lady, I'm very convinced of one thing about you. If I give you a job, I know you'll show up in the rain." He told me that there was no job opening for me at that time, but that he would call me back in a week after he created one.

At 19, on my first attempt at landing a job, I was hired to work for Delta Drilling Company in Tyler, Texas as a file clerk in the Exploration Department. My supervisor, a redhead full of energy, showed me my desk and the file room and told me to file the geologist maps in alphabetical order. My journey to working an 8 to 5 job was off to a great beginning.

I was always the first one to arrive at the office every morning and made it my responsibility to turn off the alarm, hit the lights, and make coffee. By the time the others arrived, I was already working. My supervisor would sometimes joke, "Cynthia, I like your punctuality, and I need to do better myself."

An eight-to-five for most 19-year-olds might have seemed demanding, but I was accustomed to working with my dad from six in the morning to dark, in all types of weather, so while it wasn't easy, it was far less challenging to be working in a climate-controlled office. Everything had changed for me. I went from wearing t-shirts, jeans, and boots to wearing suits. My Supervisor once told me I didn't have to wear suits with the type of job I was doing. "I'm just going to be temporarily doing this," I replied. I saw the men wearing their suits to work and figured it would be the style I'd go with.

My Supervisor encouraged and inspired me as I continued my education at Tyler Junior College. There were many times she was very blunt when correcting me, but I had developed thick skin from growing up in my household.

"Cynthia, you are such a hard worker. Where did you acquire such a work ethic?" she once asked.

"My parents taught me how to work," I told her.

Impressed with my work ethic, she told me that I needed to be doing a job more challenging than filing and answering the phone. She saw something in me that I hadn't seen in myself. She would often provide more challenging tasks for me to perform, delegate more projects for me to complete, and sometimes gave me impossible deadlines to see for herself whether I could meet them. Time after time she continued to pull gifts and abilities out of me that I was not aware I had acquired. She told me one day, "Your parents have done a fine job raising you, young lady." She never had children but treated me like the child she never had.

That summer, a secretarial position in the President's Office became available, and she encouraged me to apply for it. In order to enhance my skills and increase my qualifications, I had been attending Tyler Junior College and taking shorthand, typing, and office machines. Still, I was scared to death! In fact, both the HR manager and my supervisor encouraged me to apply for the job, and my supervisor even coached me through the interviewing process. She would drill me daily. When I would mess up, she would say let's practice tomorrow. She coached me in what to say, how to say it, and even showed me how to sit in the chair when I was talking. After all, I was a young lady used to wearing jeans and boots, and I'm sure my posture was not the best at that time.

The thought of working with the president of Delta Drilling Company scared me stiff at times, but I knew he couldn't be as strict as my dad. I kept reminding myself of this while my supervisor coached me every day. No doubt, I got the promotion and was able to experience the joy of working with a well-respected man.

With my dad having passed away, I immediately knew my responsibilities would extend to a new level, but I was eager to serve my family. I didn't consider leading a burden but something to do out of love. And, the examples set forth by my parents made knowing what to do easy. The period following my father's death was difficult for me emotionally, but the transition was smooth because my young siblings already respected my role as a leader. Karen, Anthony, and Robbie were 18, 15, and 8 respectively, all at different phases of their lives, but they were each obedient and followed the rules of the house. Because of this, I was able to help them with whatever they needed me to do in making their lives better and easier. I just wanted to spoil them like I had done with all the other children I had kept as a child.

Christmas that year without my dad was the worst I've ever experienced. Not only was I in mourning, the others in the household were experiencing enormous pain and emptiness caused by his death. I hated seeing the pain and emptiness on everyone's faces and felt helpless to do anything about it. However, easing the pressure of Christmas shopping for my mother was *one* thing I could do, and fortunately, I received a $600 bonus for Christmas. So, although my mama never asked me for money, I bought toys and presents for my sisters and brother that Christmas. I enjoyed making them happy by showering them with gifts, so whatever they wanted that Christmas, I bought it for them. It was a long, cold winter, but we survived.

CHAPTER FOUR

· · · · · · · · ● ● ● ● **●** ● ● ● ● · · · ·

Stay Focused

*"Hear counsel, and receive instruction, that thou
mayest be wise in thy latter end."* (Proverbs 19:20)

During this period, I became much more involved
in the leadership of Mt. Olive Missionary Baptist
Church. My grandmother, Lela Mae Price, had
paved the way before I was old enough to serve. She loved the
Lord and served as a faithful member of the choir. As a child, I
loved watching her sing and worship. She was barely four feet
tall and fairly plump, so it was hilarious to see her shouting
when she felt the Holy Spirit. I was able to observe and learn
from my mother, who was a youth leader, choir member, child
care provider, and announcement clerk. My grandfather, Dee
Price, served as a church leader and trustee. In fact, nearly
about all of my aunts and uncles served as leaders of Mt.

Olive. So, without anyone asking or recommending me to do so, I boldly volunteered to serve in the church.

I was now a mother and wife, holding down a full-time job, and attending college. I would have my daughter, Shayla who was now a six-year-old while Archie worked 24/7. Needless to say, that semester of college was extremely difficult, and I remember promising God, "If you help me get through the semester, I will do whatever you want me to." After graduating in December 1990, I just wanted to relax and take some time off. But no sooner had I graduated did Pastor Anthony Ruth ask me to become the church's Youth Director. Being pregnant with my son, Cameron, and experiencing both morning and evening sicknesses all the time, it was not a pleasant season in my life, so I contemplated letting some of my responsibilities go. Although I loved children, babysitting all the children of the entire church was not what I particularly had in mind. Yet, the position of Director really meant just that, Church Babysitter. So, my plate was full, and, in my mind, there was really no need to add to it. But in the end, I took my calendar out and planned activities for an entire year in about 2 hours. Thank God my teacher from high school who selected me to direct the drama production my senior year because that helped me with planning, organization, implementation, coordination, and communication.

After accepting the position, I presented the pastor a calendar the following week to make sure that it didn't conflict with any of the church's events. I had planned for the Fall Festival in October, Thanksgiving event in November, a Christmas production in December, Easter production in March, Youth Month in April, Mother's Day and graduation ceremonies in May, a trip to the Baptist Convention and Father's Day in June, Vacation Bible School in July, and a Six Flags Trip in August. To be honest, I was not concerned whether my calendar would conflict with the church's because I knew it like the back of my hand. I was just setting a professional tone. Pastor Ruth was so impressed, though, that he rewarded me with more on my plate. Over the years, I ended up serving as a choir member, bible teacher, Usher board member, Vacation Bible School leader, the Announcement Clerk and leading in the Women's Ministry. Many were amazed at how I could do so much at one time. I knew it was God's grace and favor on my life.

Adjusting to the role of the Youth Director was not easy. At times, it felt like being in a boxing ring. "We are troubled on every side, yet not distressed; we are perplexed, but not in despair." (2 Corinthians 4:8) Paul informs us that although we may think of ourselves as being helplessly at the end of the rope, we are never at the end of hope. All of our knockdowns from challenges and trials are opportunities for Christ to demonstrate his power and presence in and through us. I am sure that we all have felt like we have been knocked down a time or two while serving others yet look at yourself—we survived! I am grateful that my daughter, Shayla, started this journey with me at the age of six. She was able to sit outside the ring many days and watch me get knocked down only to get back up again. Shayla was my cheerleader!

In the Ring (First Test)

The scheduled time for choir rehearsal was 11 a.m. every third Saturday of the month. I would arrive at 10:30 a.m. so I could open the church and prepare. But time after time, my daughter and I would wait well past eleven for the musician, parents, and children to start trickling in. Each rehearsal seemed to start later than the one before until we were starting in the afternoon.

I don't think I'm going to put up with this type of behavior from these parents. I'm pregnant with morning sickness and I really don't feel like dealing with children, not to mention the parents. I am going to tell the pastor I have changed my mine!

"Sister Skief, why don't you give it some time?" Pastor Ruth calmly asked.

"Time?!" I screamed at the top of my lungs. "Who has time to deal with this?!"

I don't know how the conversation ended, but I must have answered, "Alright" somewhere along the line of it. I simply know I still felt like I was inside a boxing ring getting knocked down, whereas Pastor Ruth was seeing something inside of me that I wasn't.

In the Ring (The Thought of Quitting)

When our second rehearsal rolled around, I was three months pregnant, experiencing morning sickness, and already fed up with everyone connected to the youth ministry. Still, my daughter and I arrived early like before, promptly at 10:30, anticipating at least a modicum of improvement. However, it simply was not a good day in the house of the Lord. Once all the parents finally trickled into the church with their children, I lit into them with words I didn't even know existed. I spoke to the parents as if they were children themselves and must confess that it was one of my lowest moments. Yes, I went there. Maybe my hormones were in high gear. I was not only pregnant with my child but with what I know now was my destiny. I was pregnant in the natural as well as pregnant in the spirit.

So, what initially appeared like an easy task quickly changed into a horror story for me. The children I once babysat when they were toddlers were now teenagers, and I quickly realized why I would give them back to their parents once they started learning words. When I babysat them, they couldn't talk back, but now they were teenagers who had so much to say.

Despite all this, I loved the children and they loved me. Even with their awful attitudes, they loved Sister Skief. But, this was not the case on that memorable second rehearsal. I left the church that day infuriated at everyone. When I visited my mama's house to confide in her, I was emotionally distraught.

Thinking she would make sense of the situation, she simply agreed with me, adding, "If I were you, I would not fool with those parents or those children. You are pregnant, so let somebody else do it!" Strangely, I found myself disagreeing with her, too. Right then, it hit me like a ton of potatoes that giving up was not an option. We are taught in John 15:16a, "Ye have not chosen me, but I have chosen you, and ordained you, that ye should go and bring forth fruit." At that moment, I realized I had been called to be a leader. I had heard the voice of God, and I could not neglect my agreement with Him.

"I can't do that!" I quickly responded. Needless to say, by the time I left her house, she was as furious as I was.

Overwhelmed, I drove home and started planning youth activities. Yes, I still contemplated quitting and had all the excuses of why I did not want to continue stacked high in my mind, but I couldn't. "I can do all things through Christ which strengtheneth me." (Philippians 4:13) Plus, I knew quitting was not an option when doing what God has called you to do in the Kingdom.

In Jeremiah 29:11, it reads, "For I know the thoughts that I think toward you, saith the Lord, thoughts of peace, and not of evil, to give you an expected end." God assures us in saying, "for I know" is a promise from God. God's thoughts are higher and better than our thoughts. We don't know what will bring us peace and success, but God does! Don't quit because God has great things in store for those who love him. *God is faithful and God wants us to be faithful to Him.*

Now I'm in the ring again (God Called Me)

On the way home, my daughter cried to me, "All of those people at the church are mad at you, mama."

"I know," I said to her, thinking to myself how little I cared given how angry I was with them. I telephoned all my friends and told them about what had happened at the church. As friends, they were always great listeners. Truth is, even after 30 years of true friendship, they are still good listeners. But in this situation, they were all mute; they just listened to me carry on.

Finally, that evening I had another conversation with God, and an earlier conversation we had while I was in college kept popping up in my mind. Remember, I had promised God that if he helped me finish college, I would work for him forever. I had completed my degree at The University of Texas at Tyler with a Bachelor of Applied Arts and Sciences on December 14, 1990. Still, I asked God what He would have me to do. "Cynthia, the children." Not sure I heard him correctly, I asked again. "The children," he repeated.

I already knew God would confirm what He had said to me, so even though I wanted to quit, I couldn't! God had called me to work with these children. He had chosen me, and no one else, for this assignment. Leaders don't quit! Leaders fall down and get discouraged from time to time, but quitting is never an option. Yet, leadership is a lonely position. My dad would often say, "Cynthia, you don't worry about people liking you. Just make sure they respect you." Soon, there were a lot of people in the church who didn't like me, but I can't recall anyone who didn't respect me.

Round Four (God Help!)

I went to God in prayer, and it was through reading my bible and listening to God's voice that I was able to continue. But, admittedly, I was beginning to feel like Moses, " But the house of Israel will not hearken unto thee; for they will not hearken unto me." (Ezekiel 3:7a) Of course, I wasn't leading an army, just 50 children who thought they were grown.

People will forsake you. They will leave you. In fact, we ourselves have sometimes forsaken those in need of our help, trust, and prayer. I've not always been there for everyone who's needed me. Even in the most basic sense of the word, I've failed in this regard. If people got on my nerves, I was gone! I have been very guilty of forsaking and leaving people. But when you feel forsaken and alone, think about what Jesus felt when he made his triumphant entry into Jerusalem riding a donkey. The people were ecstatic. They cried, "Hosanna, Hosanna" as He rode into town, yet not more than a few days later, they were screaming, "Crucify Him, Crucify Him!" Yes, it hurt Jesus' feelings, but He knew his purpose. Yes, it hurts God's feeling when we forsake Him.

There were many times I felt forsaken by family members and people I thought loved me and were in my corner. God assures us in Deuteronomy 31:6 "Be strong and of a good courage, fear not, nor be afraid of them: for the Lord thy God, he it is that doth go with thee; he will not fail thee, nor forsake thee." As with all scripture, I believe in this verse with all my heart. Trusting these few powerful words have cause my life to change. God was preparing me to follow Him even when people weren't. Being a leader requires making decisions that others may not like or will disagree with. For this reason, I rarely trust people who God hasn't placed in my life to be trusted.

Round Five (Establish Standards)

The next meeting, I was prepared with the agenda. But this meeting was much different from the previous ones. For one, I was taking God at his word. My daughter and I arrived early and started the meeting promptly at 11 am. A few minutes after eleven, she complained, "Mama, the people are not here yet." I told her God was here with us and it was time to get started. Although the parents and children arrived late as usual, I continued with my agenda, which included several items. I didn't even mention their tardiness, but, at the end of the meeting, encouraged them to be on time in the future, adding, "Because I will be starting on time with or without you." A standard had been established. *Leaders decide to lead, or the people will lead you.*

Establishing a positive and respectful culture in our youth ministry took a few months, but eventually everyone was on the same page. It was a process. In my daily conversation with God, I now began confessing, "In all thy ways acknowledge him, and he shall direct thy paths." (Proverbs 3:6) God was now clearing a pathway to success for me and the children he had entrusted me with.

In the end, I was able to work with some of the most amazing men and women on earth. I served as Youth Director at Mt. Olive Missionary Baptist Church for 10 years, and during this period, the parents were eager to get involved with all activities. All special events became a rewarding time for the entire congregation. I delegated and allowed other volunteers with special gifts to have ownership in their involvement, and the youth looked forward to the big productions each year (especially Black History, Easter, and Christmas). The most rewarding productions were the Easter and Christmas pageantries, where I was able to involve the entire congregation. There were volunteers that built sets, erected the cross, organized the costumes, and prepared all the other items called for. By now, my fear of speaking before large audiences was no longer a problem. However, it was a lot better delegating the Easter speeches to others than having to deliver them myself.

During those 10 years, with Mt. Olive's' youth, I discovered my gift of discerning special talent in others. Further, I learned how to allow talented individuals to operate, blossom, and shine. After reading a script, I would already know which child would be playing certain parts.

Parents would often say, "Sister Skief, how did you know how to select the children for the parts?"

"It's a gift from God," was my typical response.

I could role play with the children if they struggled with their lines or speeches. The parents would share with me that they were unable to get their children to learn the speeches and wondered how I could motivate them to perform at such a high level. The answer was simple. I would set a standard of excellence and the children responded accordingly every time. I still smile when I think about the struggles we encountered initially and how God changed the situation and began granting us miracle after miracle. *Every move you make, every turn you take, whether you open your mouth or not, you will impact someone's life because someone is watching you.*

CHAPTER FIVE

· · · · · · ●●●● ● ●●●● · · · · ·

Stepping into Leadership

"Take fast hold of instruction; let her not go: keep
her; for she is thy life." (Proverbs 4:13)

While employed as an administrative assistant
for the Director of Human Resources at the
University of Texas Health Center at Tyler,
I was told by my supervisor that I would be facilitating
orientation for all new employees. I immediately thought to
myself, *I don't want to do that.* As if reading my mind, she added,
"Get ready." My knees were shaking, and I literally thought I
was going to get choked. But every month, it became easier,
and I eventually became a great public speaker. My supervisor
knew I was nervous at first, but she saw something in me I
hadn't seen in myself.

When I left my position, I received many calls from the workers who came after me and the staff members still employed there. I was talented but also arrogant and had an attitude problem. God had gifted me with many talents. In all honesty, I really didn't know I had so many gifts until I would go on vacation. Then, the staff would call me every day. But even when I quit that job, the staff continued to call me, and they ended up replacing me with 3 people.

The new people would telephone and email me to get my advice on solving problems. They would always ask how I did all of the work, not understanding that God had anointed me and given me grace for the assignments. God did not anoint them to do my assignments any more than he anointed me to do their assignments. Still, most watched but could not figure out how I easily accomplished so much in such a short time. What they didn't understand was that I made things look easy because of God's grace.

The tailor who made Aaron's garments was given wisdom by God in order to do *his* task. All of us have special skills. My garment was not designed or tailored for anyone else to wear but me. God wants to fill us with his Spirit so we will use our talents for his glory. Think about your special talents and abilities and the ways you could use them for God's work in the world. A talent must be used, or it will diminish. I had an anointing to perform at a level that was not the norm for others. Many tried but did not realize that God had made that garment just for me. Because God has given all of us special talents and abilities, I have never tried to be like others. We should always strive to be our best at what *we* do.

Ask yourself, what can you do to bring God glory. God wants your gift for His glory. Again, God uses your gifts for His glory! Therefore, our gifts and talents should not be taken lightly. Where God gives the vision, He will provide the provision and open up doors that men cannot close.

In 2003, I decided to give up my career to pursue God and fulfill my God-given plan. I wanted to bring God glory in all that I did for the Kingdom because only what you do for Christ will last. At times, it was tough for our family, but God always made a way for us. Sometimes, it seemed as though he was squeezing water out of a rock for us. Most people didn't know that we were struggling, and at the time, we also felt we had lost a lot. However, when I look back on all the wonderful things God has given us, we only profited. God was shaping me and molding me into a leader who could stand strong and trust in His power.

Heavenly Father, thank you for giving me all that I need from day to day. Father, today I want to live for you and make the Kingdom of God my priority. In Jesus name, Amen.

CHAPTER SIX

· · · · · · ● ● ● ◉ ● ● ● · · · ·

Leadership at a Crossroad

"Buy the truth, and sell it not; also, wisdom, and instruction, and understanding." (Proverbs 23:23)

Archie and I were the perfect parents for raising our children. When they were small, he worked nights, and I worked days. Both of us were very organized and liked a clean house, so when I worked during the day, Archie not only prepared dinner for the family, fixed the diaper bags, refilled the baby's milk bottles, and organized their clothes for the next day, he also completed anything that I left undone. We both had great work ethics, and prior to him suffering two strokes, he was the type who did whatever it took to provide for his family. He remains the best father any child could ask for, loving and supportive, and is always cheering us on. He is always aware of what we are doing so that he can encourage and support us.

Looking back, I could never tell that we were so busy because Archie always kept things organized for us at home. When the children became teenagers, they had chores, but Archie would make sure their rooms were always clean. Shayla and Cameron were both very active in school sports and band activities, so, unless Archie or I had to work, our evenings were always filled during the week. We never had a date night alone because our children always wanted to hang out with us, probably out of fear they'd miss out on an opportunity to eat out. Eating out was always a fun activity for our family, but the most important activity we did as a family was to celebrate our wins, talk about our losses, and discuss how we could do better the next week.

Nevertheless, the nineties decade was a season of my life full of volatility and challenges. Soon after the birth of Cameron, my son, in 1992, God began to change my life. There wasn't any particular cliff-hanging event, rather a slow back and forth process. It was a period of being with and without God, and this indecisiveness went on for several years. In fact, the nineties were a dark period for many of us, even if we weren't aware of it. There was a spike in crime, and drug use was rampant, especially in neighborhoods like mine across the country.

By 1998, I became fed up. I didn't feel safe inside my own home anymore, and with Archie working the nightshift, it was often just me and the children at home alone. Because of the drugs and crime infesting our neighborhood, I encouraged Archie to move our family as far away as possible. So, we soon moved into a beautiful new home in Flint, Texas. But what looked like a picture-perfect family was instead a broken and dysfunctional one simply masquerading the drama.

In 2000, while training for a new job in Tyler Texas, a young lady I had gotten acquainted with wanted to share a cassette tape with me. I was down that day wearing a smile in the midst of adversity, but she saw straight through all the pain and suffering I was experiencing and offered the best help she could. I got in my car and drove home listening to a tape of the renowned evangelist Dr. Tony Evans. The title of his message was *Are You Going to Let the Devil Win?* Ironically, that's exactly how I felt that day, like the devil was winning in every area of my family's life. I remember ejecting the cassette and flipping in Whitney Houston's "Heartbreak Hotel," which was climbing all the charts. I simply wasn't in the mood to listen to Evan's message that day.

Archie had a day off that Sunday and was taking the kids to the country to visit his mother. After they left, I put the cassette tape in to listen to the message so that I could return it to the young lady on Monday. This time, Evans' voice began to penetrate the walls of our home: "Are you going to let the devil have your marriage? Are you going to let the devil have your children? Are you quitting? If you allow the devil to have your marriage, you are simply allowing the devil to win! If you allow the devil to have your children, you are simply allowing him to win! Are you a quitting? Are you throwing in the towel and saying, devil you win?" The power of the Holy Spirit rose up on the inside of me, and I begin to shout throughout my home, "Devil, you will not win! You can't have my marriage, and you can't have my children!" I really didn't know exactly what had happened, but something changed that day.

I could not wait until my family returned home. I apologized to Archie and told him I had not given up on our family. I told him that the Holy Spirit had spoken to me and I was not going to allow the devil to have our marriage. He was as puzzled as I was. Soon, we were back to being happy and encouraged. I began to pray more often and sought God for the answers I needed. I was hungry and thirsty for the word of God. I began reading my bible and regularly listening to Evans' messages. Still, something was missing.

Although God had promised that He would never leave or forsake me, I still felt forsaken by certain people in my life. The following Sunday, I didn't feel worthy of teaching Sunday School because I hadn't lived up to the standards put forth in the bible. I knew my faith was not complete, and I was the type of person who wouldn't teach what I hadn't lived or was failing at. Honestly, I did not want God to strike me down in the church for being a hypocrite. To make matters worse, the lesson was "God will Never Leave You or Forsake You." I definitely wasn't feeling that at all, so I did not teach that lesson. Later, while sitting in the choir behind the pastor during the sermon, I thought I would casually do my grocery list. Yes, I was planning on ignoring the sermon, too.

Mt. Olive's Pastor, Reverend Daryl McNealy, was a really great and outstanding preacher, but I wasn't feeling him at all on this Sunday. The more I seemed to be ignoring him, though, the louder he became. "God will never leave you nor forsake you!" he kept repeating. I thought, *Oh my God, here we go again!* The Pastor got right in my face and shouted again, "God said, Sister Skief, that He would never leave you nor forsake you!"

Before I knew it, I had leapt from my seat and began to cry, stretching my hands to the ceiling and hollering, "Yes, Lord, Yes, Lord, Yes, Lord!" I shouted all over that choir loft, as I was filled with the Holy Spirit. Something changed in my life that day.

The songs that I had sung unto the Lord, all the prayers I had cried unto the Lord, and all hurt that I had felt—it felt like God was holding me in His arms, showing me how much He loved me. I felt loved that day! I felt restored that day! Occasionally some of the elderly people would tell me how I looked like a different person. "Sister you are full of the Holy Ghost, and God has His hand upon you, sister." I knew that God was changing me from the inside out. The gifts and talents were being refined and my character and leadership skills were crystallizing into fruition.

CHAPTER SEVEN

· · · · · · ● ● ● ● ● ● ◉ ● ● ● ● ● · · ·

Pursuing the Internal Leader

"All scripture is given by inspiration of God, and is profitable for doctrine, for reproof, for correction, for instruction in righteousness." (2 Timothy 3:16)

I am going to be very transparent with you, so get ready. Had it not been for God's saving grace and mercy that followed me all the days of my life, I would be completely lost, unable to help myself let alone anyone else. Before making a decision to lead, I should have been a better student of the bible. For example, I should have understood, "The fruit of the Spirit is love, joy, peace, longsuffering, gentleness, goodness, faith, Meekness, temperance: against such there is no law." (Galatians 5:22-23) Yes, God equips those he calls to lead with the above characteristics. I absolutely did not have any patience, nor did I understand how to be gentle.

Longsuffering? What was that? I would give you about 5 minutes of my time, then your time was up! I possessed no self-control and would curse people out at the drop of a dime. Only after I finished saying what I had to say could I fathom the notion of self-restraint. If I thought you loved me, I loved you. If I thought you was good to me, I was good to you. But God was calling me to be a leader? Why, you might ask?

I was the type of leader nobody was going to follow anywhere, and I wouldn't blame them since I didn't want to follow me either. I was leading like I had seen others do. I had been taught by my dad, who liked to often say, "Don't ask questions, just do as I say." Although there were many good leaders in my life, there were a lot of not-so-good ones. I simply did not know how to lead and was messed up on the inside trying to. I appeared to be ready, dressed and looked the part, but was internally messed up. There were things inside of me that were not good. Every night, I would always talk to the Holy Spirit and repent for all my sins before the Lord. I would ask God to wash me with the blood of Jesus. One night, I could not stop singing, "Please, Search Me Lord - If you find anything that shouldn't be, please take it out and cleanse me, because I want to be right, I want to be saved and I've got to be whole." I would passionately sing that song and sincerely wanted to be changed. James Cleveland's Something's "Got

A hold on Me" was another song I sang: "I went to a meeting one night, and my heart wasn't right, something… got a hold on me, oh yes it did, I say something… Got a hold on me. It was the Holy Ghost, Holy Ghost, yeah, the Holy Ghost."

I not only sang but persistently prayed. I prayed that God would take the cursing off my tongue, and he began to hear my cries. That's when I knew God was real in my life. God began to change me from the inside out. I asked God, *Would you please demonstrate your power in my life?* It was then that I knew he really wanted me to be a Bible teacher. God did it! One day Archie was upset and yelled a curse word. I immediately responded, "Don't say that!"

"Oh, since you don't curse anymore, now you can correct everyone else?" Archie asked rhetorically, already having noticed the change in me, just waiting for the right moment to tell me.

I had stopped cursing and didn't even know it, but my family did! I made a vow to my Savior, Jesus Christ, "If you would teach me how to love and forgive, then I would love and forgive, but I can't do it on my own." Again, God did it! I began to love the people like God wanted me to love and forgive as He would have us to. *A prayer that I pray often: Father teach me to love people the way you love; teach me to forgive people the way you forgive; teach me to see people the way you see them; and, teach me to see myself the way you see me. In Jesus name, Amen*

God already knows our sins and shortcomings. God is not in Heaven with a giant stick waiting for us to make a mistake so he can beat us with it. God is waiting for us to confess our sins so that we will be healed on the inside. "That if thou shalt confess with thy mouth the Lord Jesus, and shalt believe in thine heart that God hath raised him from the dead, thou shalt be saved." (Roman 10:9) The healing begins when we confront and confess our sins to Him. There is no crime or sin that God can't be forgiven by God. We can go boldly to our Father and ask Him to forgive us. Because he loves us unconditionally, He is just waiting to forgive us.

In Hebrews 4:16, it reads: "Let us therefore come boldly unto the throne of grace that we may obtain mercy and find grace to help in time of need." I needed God's grace and mercy! It's available, and I'm asking you to not waste any more time and come boldly unto the throne of grace! God will meet you right where you are. Broken, wounded, hurt, disappointed, discouraged, depressed, oppressed, angry, or feeling stuck—God is ready to give you grace and mercy. God loves you!

Sin comes with a price. When I was losing my family, Satan was able to laugh at me. When I was losing with the members at church, losing with co-workers, and the enemy was trying to take me out, Satan felt comfortable belittling me. However, when I confessed my sins and my shortcoming, when I confessed that I had no patience before God, and when I asked God to help me with my longsuffering, Satan had to step back.

If it had not been for my mother teaching me the 23 Psalm, I would have not known how to confess my sins. I recite the Lord's prayer and Psalm 23 daily. I remember teaching it to the youth, and one parent had the nerve to say to me, "Is that the only scriptures you know?" In many instances, such a comment would have angered me. Yes, I was shocked by her question, but God had already changed my heart, and I was not about to bend to her level. Indeed, I would instruct the youth to recite the Lord's Prayer and Psalm 23 before each of their services. No, it was not the only scripture I knew, but the Lord's Prayers and Psalm 23 were significant for me and the youth during this time.

I have mentioned these scriptures because they renewed my spirit and mind on a daily basis. My heart became more loving, I learned how to forgive others, and, most importantly, I was cultivating a relationship with my Lord and Savior Jesus Christ.

CHAPTER EIGHT

· · · · · ● ● ● ● ● ● ● ● ● · · · ·

Accepting Leadership Responsibility

*"Give instruction to a wise (WO) man, and (s) he)
will be yet wiser: teach a just (WO) man, and (s)
he will increase in learning. (Adjustments (WO)
(s) to read for a woman)."* (Proverbs 9:9)

The fruit of the Spirit is the spontaneous work of the Holy Spirit in us. The Spirit produces the character traits found in the nature of Christ. They are the by-products of Christ's control—we can't obtain them by trying to get them without his help. If we want the fruit of the Spirit to grow in us, we must join our life to his "Abide in me, and I in you. As the branch cannot bear fruit of itself, except it abide in the vine; no more can ye, except ye abide in me. I am the vine, ye are the branches: He that abideth in me, and I in him, the same bringeth forth much fruit: for without me ye can do nothing." (John 15:4-5). We must know him, love him, remember him, and imitate him. When we do this, we will fulfill the intended purpose of the law—to love God and our neighbors. Which of these qualities do you want the Spirit to produce in you?

I knew God had called me to take up a leadership role. More so, I realized that without God's guidance, I was going to lead all of us to hell quickly. God's help is indispensable, without it we are destined to fail. I wanted to be a great leader, yet I wanted to get it right. I did not want to pattern after some of the leadership I had experienced at church or at work.

By allowing the Holy Spirit to work on the inner me, I am able to exude leadership character traits God intended for us to have. The Holy Spirit helps me daily with patience. My daughter remembered how I had started out as a leader with the youth and the parents and she could witness the change God had made in my life. After a very intense and heated meeting with the parents of my youth, I can remember my daughter telling me that God had changed me. When God changes you on the inside, others will see the evidence of the working miracle God produces in your life.

I began to pray for God to take out all the things inside of me that did not bring him glory. The Holy Spirit taught me how to love, forgive, and be gentle with my enemies. Most importantly, he taught me to have longsuffering with my enemies.

While I was screaming, "God, change those children, and please change those parents," God was not interested. He was only interested in changing Cynthia Skief. God had called me to be the leader filled with the fruit, and when I finally began asking God to change me, He did! When I was Youth Director, God taught me how to be an assertive leader instead of an aggressive one, an effective and efficient leader, and a planner with excellent organizational skills filled with the fruits of the Spirit. When God developed me as a leader with the fruits of the spirit, I was able to train, develop, and nurture leaders around me. I could not give them what I had not received myself, and I realized that to be a great leader, you must first be a great follower, teachable, and a student of the Bible. I have been a faithful follower with the best of them and the worst of them, yet God always granted us with grace and mercy during those times.

I am called to serve. I am eager to serve, and as for me and my house, we will serve the Lord all the days of our life. I am humbled to be chosen by God, and my best days are still ahead of me. *"When I am talking, I am teaching. When I am listening, I am learning."*

CHAPTER NINE

· · · · · · ● ● ● ● ● ● ● ● ● · · · · · ·

A Born Passion to Lead

"Now the Lord had said unto Abram, Get thee out of thy country, and from thy kindred, and from thy father's house, unto a land that I will shew thee: And I will make of thee a great nation, and I will bless thee, and make thy name great; and thou shalt be a blessing: And I will bless them that bless thee, and curse him that curseth thee: and in thee shall all families of the earth be blessed." (Genesis 12:1-3)

My story sounds a lot like Abram's story. I never asked anyone what they thought about me moving to Houston. I heard the voice and command from God, and that was all I needed.

When my season was up at my home church, Mt. Olive Missionary Baptist Church in Winona, Texas, I began to ask God where my family should go from there. It was a hard season, and I was broken in many areas of my life.

One day, while on an extended fast, a young lady from work gave me a cassette tape to listen to. That week, we had shared with each other how music healed and gave you answers. During lunch, I put the cassette tape in my SUV, and the lyrics of a song by Tramaine Hawkins began to play:

> In case you have fallen by the wayside of life
> dreams and visions shattered; you're all broken
> inside.

> You don't have to stay in the shape that you're in
> the potter wants to put you back together again
> oh, the potter wants to put you back together
> again.

I began to weep. I played the song three times and each time I wept. But I received my answer. I shared with my family that we would be attending church at The Potter's House, and the next week, my husband, Archie Skief, gave his life to Christ in our home. That Sunday, September 2000, we joined The Potter's House as a family. When I was in darkness, Bishop Jakes was the light God shined on our lives in order for us to see. His sermons, the Pastors and Leaders Conferences, Woman Thou Art Loosed Conferences, God's Leading Ladies Conference, Invocation Conferences, yearly revivals, and Wednesday Night Bible Classes all played a role in me becoming the strong and courageous leader that I am today. The spiritual guidance, along with my parental guidance, paved the way for me as a leader. There were times that I felt like Bishop Jakes and I grew up in the same house. Because of his life experiences. I am forever grateful to one of the most powerful preachers in the world, Bishop T.D. Jakes, Senior Pastor at The Potter's House in Dallas Texas. He is one of the greatest pastors, teachers, and preachers we have on earth. However, God never released me to serve at The Potter's House.

After attending Bishop Jakes' church, in November 2003, I was ordained as a minister to preach the gospel. With my husband and children supporting me, I began preaching in my home in April 2004. Archie would awaken every Sunday morning and prepare our living room for church service. Every Saturday night, I would say to God, "If you don't speak, I don't have anything to say to your people." For a year, the Spirit of God would come upon me at midnight with a word. After service, I would often contact my friend attending The Potter's House and ask her what Bishop Jakes preached about. She would share his scripture and message, and on many Sundays, Bishop Jakes and I were on the same page. God was confirming that I was on the right path.

But after one year, God stopped speaking, and I stopped preaching because I didn't have anything to say. So, I went on a fast to receive God's guidance for our family. It was during this time that my friend invited me to attend a new multiracial church in Tyler. I attended a Saturday night service and listened to Tommy Tenney, who was there for the ministry's grand opening. His message, based on a scripture from I Kings 17:2-8, was that God would feed you while you were supposed to be in a certain place. When it was your time to move on, the brook would dry up, and God would direct you to another place for a supply of food.

The Spirit of God came upon me, and I knew New Life Worship Center was our new place to worship. I went home and told my family that New Life Worship Center was going to be our new church home. How many people do you know of joining a church before hearing the Pastor preach? The next Sunday, we went to hear Pastor Rudy Bond deliver a stirring sermon.

We joined as a family in June 2005. I served in leadership in many capacities (Elder/Deaconess, Women Ministry Leader, Bible Teacher Facilitator, Coordinator of Events, Easter and Christmas Production Leader for the children and Executive Council Leader). I had the opportunity to work as the administrative assistant to Pastors Rudy and C.J. Bond. My favorite part of this job was typing Pastor Bond's sermons.

On the days leading up to my birthday in 2012, I always fast. This time, I sensed a move coming on, so I shared it with Archie and the children. I even told the Landlord I sensed a move coming on but didn't know when it would be. I continued to fast and seek God's guidance about the move I was sensing. I even shared it with Pastor Bond, who told me, "With a vision like that, you will need a Pastor like Bishop T.D. Jakes or Pastor Joel Osteen to fulfill your purpose!"

I also like to fast right before Christmas and the new year. Strangely enough, during this month of December I began seeing the word Houston everywhere. One day while shopping in the store and I saw this lady with her baby. I asked, "What's your baby's name?" She replied, "Houston." I was even invited to Houston for the week of Christmas to keep my adopted grandchildren. While visiting, the Spirit of God came upon me and I began to weep. I knew what that meant. The Holy Spirit confirmed that Houston would be our new home. I called Archie on December 28, 2012 while I was still there and asked him how he liked the sound of Houston being our new home. He concurred, so I drove home and began to pack. The move did not set well with a few of my family members, but it was not their destiny that God had spoken to—it was mine.

We moved to Rosenberg, where, for several months, we assisted a pastor who was building a ministry there. However, I soon realized this ministry was not what God was calling me to do and began to act like one of the Israelites, "God why did you bring me here?" I was very uncomfortable in this ministry, but we kept on trusting God. I kept asking God why we had to move so fast. My answer came during Memorial Day weekend, when we learned that my brother had stage 4 throat cancer. That year, I traveled back and forth from Winona to Dallas to be with my brother and family until I finally asked God, "Do I need to move back to Tyler?" The answer came so fast, I don't really know whether I completed my question. Yet, I traveled back to Houston with so many questions.

I found myself repeatedly asking God, *Where do we go from here in our search for a church home in Houston?* It was time to fast and pray. In July, my friend, Ula was visiting me in Houston. I took her on a tour of the town, and as we drove down highway 59 South toward Rosenberg, I pointed toward Lakewood Church and informed her, "Lakewood is the largest church in Houston." As I kept my eyes on the highway, hers remained on Lakewood. "Cynthia," she shouted, not taking her eyes off the huge church building, "I see you all up in there serving and worshiping God."

"Stop that!" I replied, laughing. "Girl, I went there for the Woman Thou Art Loose Conference and sat in the nose bleed section, near the flag in the back of the church."

"I don't see you in the back. You will be at the front," she quickly responded. "I see you all around those windows praying."

Once again, I told her to stop that! We laughed. She then announced, "Girl, you better get ready! I feel the Spirit of God all over me!"

I did, too. However, I didn't want to hear that from her because I needed to hear the voice of God for myself. It did seem, however, that every time I transitioned to another ministry, God always used Ula to confirm God's will for me.

August is a special time of the year for me, as it is the month of my birth. I always take a few days during this month to fast, pray, and seek God's direction on the path my husband and I should be taking. Archie and I were especially in need of direction in our search for a new church home. One night, I was shopping for groceries at HEB and noticed one of Jentezen Franklin's books, *Fasting the Cutting Edge,* displayed on a kiosk. I purchased a copy and began reading while completing my own personal 21 day fast. It wasn't long into the fast, although, when I received a revelation. God told me to turn on the television and flip the channel to TBN. I did as I was told, and there sat Pastor Joel Osteen across the table from Paul and Jan Crouch. I had never followed Pastor Joel's ministry, but God told me then that I would meet him and his wife, Victoria.

Shortly after completing my fast, about 3 days later, I got a call from Lakewood Church. I pulled the phone away from my ear to ask myself, "Is this Lakewood Church, for real?" I listened to the recording, which announced that Jentezen Franklin was going to be speaking on Saturday night at 7 pm and at the 8:30 and 11 a.m. services on Sunday. I remember thinking to myself, "God, how did Lakewood Church get my phone number, and how did they know I had just finished reading his book?" I knew God was up to something.

I attended Lakewood Church that Saturday night and informed the friendly individual who greeted me at the entrance that it was my first time attending a service. The Greeter ushered me to the front of the church. I told the

Usher that I was new and was wondering whether I could sit in the front row. He looked puzzled but recovered quickly.

"Let me see what I can do." About ten minutes later, he returned to ask me whether I still wanted to sit in the front row.

"Yes," I said.

So, there I sat, front and center. I gazed to the right and realized Mama Dodie, Jentezen Franklin, and Pastor Joel were seated just a few seats down on the same row. I whispered to myself, "God, for real? Is this really happening to me?" Franklin's message was totally for me, and I'll never forget the moment he said, "Some of you are wondering where home is. Well, God is speaking and saying welcome home!" I began to weep because I knew I had found my new church home. Pastor Joel talked to the audience afterwards and reminded us, "If you attend 3 services, you will officially be a Lakewood member," so I attended all 3 services that weekend.

I shared with my husband that Lakewood Church was our new church home. Already a member, I was still eager to hear Pastor Joel preach the following Sunday. The next Sunday we attended the morning service to hear our new pastors for the first time. Archie immediately fell in love with Pastor Joel's humor. Osteen is known for telling a joke prior to delivering each sermon. There was a pastor close to death and he requested that the lawyer and IRS agent sit next to him. They both were delighted that the pastor had requested them to sat next to him. The lawyer mustered up enough nerve to ask the pastor why he requested them to sit next to him. The pastor said that Jesus died between two thieves and that is the way I want to go.

I am currently serving as a Prayer Partner Co-Leader, Stephen Minister Facilitator, Women Ministry/Better Together Facilitator, Business Ministry Team Volunteer and Pastor's Visitor Reception Line for 2 services on Sunday at one of the largest churches in the United States. Sunday mornings are the only day I set my alarm clock for 5:30 a.m. I am not a morning person, but Sunday mornings are my divine mornings to praise and worship the Lord publicly. I never dreamed of being at one of the largest churches in the United States.

My brother, Anthony Quinn Cooper, went home to be with the Lord November 21, 2013. As I was driving back to Houston, God spoke to me, "If I had not moved you so fast and had you heard your brother had cancer, Cynthia, you wouldn't have heard my voice, and you wouldn't have left Tyler." I cried. Grieving the loss of a brother isn't something any person is prepared for, so the next few months would be very difficult for me. In my case, it was Anthony who gave me my first opportunities to lead. Now I couldn't tell him what to do anymore. "Cynt thinks she everybody's Mama, the boss, trying to tell everybody what to do!" That's where I got my start as a leader. However, I am really just getting started.

AFTERWORD

· · · · · ● ● ● ● ● ● ● ● ● ● · · · ·

"For I know the thoughts that I think toward you,
saith the Lord, thoughts of peace, and not of evil, to
give you an expected end." (Jeremiah 29:11)

Accoding to Jeremiah, God has a plan for you. God has placed a leader inside all of us. It requires allowing the Master leader to lead and teach you. It requires allowing God to be your GPS from day to day. It requires that you be obedient to God's voice and not follow that of strangers. God knows what's best for you and me. He knows the best way for you to reach your destiny. In fact, he has already cleared the path for you to walk. He knows the right timing to bring you to a successful place. It does not matter when you start, where you start, or how you start. What's important is that you start and allow God to be the author of your destiny. Be encouraged that your footsteps are directed by God and trust Him even when you can't trace

Him; trust Him when it seems dark. Trust Him for the right timing.

God loves you so much!

Here are some ways to stay Together

Http://www.cynthiaskief.com

Instagram: cynthiaskief

Facebook: A Born Leader – Author, Cynthia Skief

NOTES

_____

_____

_____

_____

_____

_____

_____

_____

_____

_____

_____

_____

_____

_____

_____

_____

NOTES

_____

_____

_____

_____

_____

_____

_____

_____

_____

_____

_____

_____

_____

_____

_____

_____

_____

NOTES

NOTES

_____

_____

_____

_____

_____

_____

_____

_____

_____

_____

_____

_____

_____

_____

_____

_____

_____

NOTES

_____

_____

_____

_____

_____

_____

_____

_____

_____

_____

_____

_____

_____

_____

_____

NOTES

_____

_____

_____

_____

_____

_____

_____

_____

_____

_____

_____

_____

_____

_____

_____

_____

_____

NOTES

43994127R00063

Made in the USA
Lexington, KY
05 July 2019